# The BIG BOOK of Mobiles
# Bugs

## How to make your mobiles

You will need some thread, string, or monofilament to hang your mobiles.

**1** You will find the mobiles inside this book attached to pages 6 and 7, and pages 10 and 11. Carefully detach the mobile pages along the perforated edges.

**2** Press out all the mobile illustrations, except the pieces marked A, B, C, and D. Cut pieces of thread a few inches long (or longer if desired). Tie the thread to the mobile pieces by pushing the ends of the thread into the slits and winding them around at least three times.

**3** Press out one part of the hanger, marked A. Following the positions shown in the diagrams, assemble the mobile pieces and tie them to A.

**A. Flying bugs**          **A. Ground bugs**

**4** Now follow step 3 for the second part of the hanger, marked B. Tie a thread to the top of B.

**B. Flying bugs**          **B. Ground bugs**

     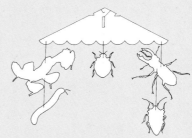

**5** Assemble the hanger by fitting A and B together. Following this diagram, slide A into B through the diagonal slit in B.

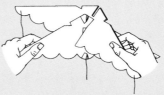

**6** Press out the ring marked C. Pass the thread from the top of B through the center of the ring. Gently press C onto the top of the hanger until the four points of the X-shaped hole fit into notches cut in the hanger.

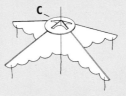

**7** Press out the hook marked D and attach it to the thread from the top of the hanger. You can use the hook to hang up your mobile.

TIME
LIFE®
BOOKS

# The world of bugs

IN EVERY HOUSE, garden, field, or forest on Earth, there is a world full of activity which we hardly even notice. In the soil, in the air, and in the water, live many kinds of "bugs"—insects, spiders, and other minute animals.

There are more different species of insects than any other animal group. Scientists think there are at least five million species, probably more. There is a fantastic variety of shapes, sizes, and colors, but all insects have the same basic design. Every insect has three pairs of legs and a skeleton on the outside of its body. There are three parts to its body: the head, the thorax, which bears the legs and wings, and the abdomen. An insect breathes through tiny holes in its sides. Many insects have wings.

Look carefully in a small area of soil and you will discover hundreds of bugs. Not all of them are insects: spiders, which have eight legs and two body parts, are arachnids; millipedes and centipedes have many body parts and legs; and woodlice are crustaceans, related to crabs.

**Water bear or tardigrade**
*Up to 0.02 in. long*
*Worldwide*

## Mini-monster

The tiny **water bear** lives in the thin film of water covering some plants. Under a microscope, we can see the "claws" on its feet.

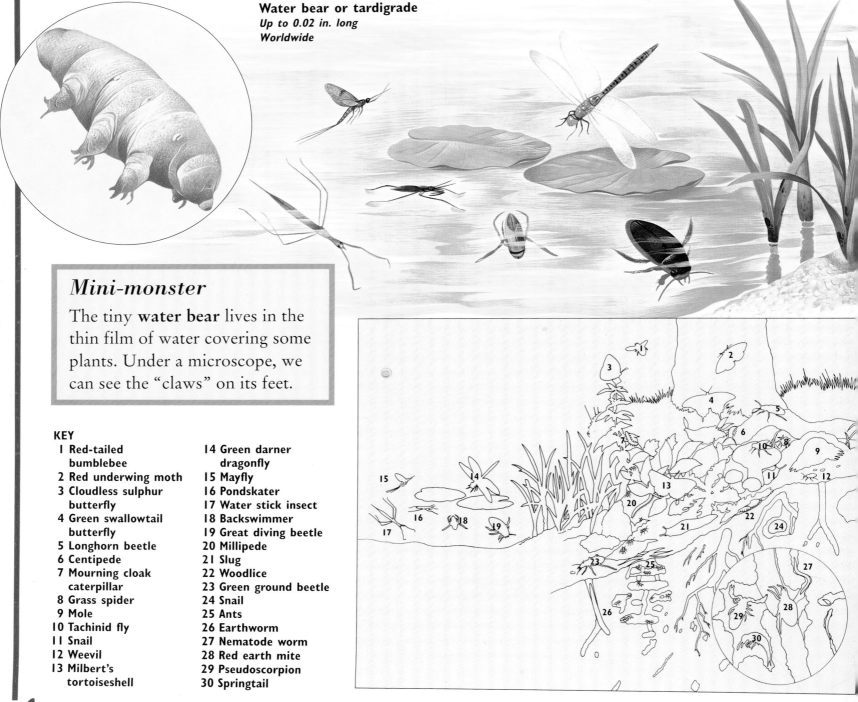

**KEY**

1 Red-tailed bumblebee
2 Red underwing moth
3 Cloudless sulphur butterfly
4 Green swallowtail butterfly
5 Longhorn beetle
6 Centipede
7 Mourning cloak caterpillar
8 Grass spider
9 Mole
10 Tachinid fly
11 Snail
12 Weevil
13 Milbert's tortoiseshell
14 Green darner dragonfly
15 Mayfly
16 Pondskater
17 Water stick insect
18 Backswimmer
19 Great diving beetle
20 Millipede
21 Slug
22 Woodlice
23 Green ground beetle
24 Snail
25 Ants
26 Earthworm
27 Nematode worm
28 Red earth mite
29 Pseudoscorpion
30 Springtail

**Luna moth**
*Wingspan 3–4.25 in.*
*North America*

## Incredible journey

The **monarch butterfly** lives for almost a year, and during that time makes one truly amazing journey. In late summer, the butterfly leaves the area in Canada or the northern U.S. where it hatched. It flies all the way to California or Mexico to hibernate for the winter. This can be a distance of 2,000 miles. It spends the winter clinging to a tree with thousands of others, so that the tree looks as if it is covered by an orange blanket. Then, as spring arrives, the butterflies start their long journey home.

## Magnificent moths

The **luna moth,** or **North American moon moth,** gets its name from the markings on its wings. They look just like crescent moons. The luna moth's long wing tails make it easily recognizable.

One insect that is difficult to ignore is the **hercules moth.** As a caterpillar, it is large, spiky, and brightly colored. When it becomes an adult, it really is a giant. Its wings are wider than this page!

**Monarch butterfly**
*Wingspan 3–4 in.*
*North America*

**Purple emperor butterfly**
*Wingspan 2.5–3 in.*
*Europe, Asia*

**Hercules moth caterpillar**
*Up to 6.75 in. long*
*Australia, Southeast Asia*

# Flying bugs mobile

**Burnet moth**
*Wingspan 1.5 in.*
*Europe, Asia*

**Cecropia moth**
*Wingspan 6 in.*
*North America*

## Warning colors

Unlike many dull, night-flying moths, the **burnet moth** is brightly colored. It flies about in the daylight, and rests out in the open. However, the burnet moth is in little danger from attack, because its bright colors warn predators that it is poisonous.

## Amazing senses

The **cecropia moth,** a kind of silkmoth, has special featherlike antennae which provide it with its most important sense, smell. A male can detect a female from several miles away! The antennae have many branches, each with thousands of tiny hairs picking up scents. The moth is provided with information about possible food sources.

A species of silkmoth has been bred in special farms in China, India, and Japan for centuries. Its caterpillars ("silk worms") produce silk to make cocoons.

**Indian leaf butterfly**
*Wingspan 4.75 in.*
*South and East Asia*

**European cockchafer**
*1 in. long*

## Hiding from danger

This side of the **Indian leaf butterfly's** wings could not be more colorful. However, if the butterfly closed its wings, you would be surprised to see something that looked like an old brown leaf. Like other butterflies, the Indian leaf butterfly hides its bright colors while it is at rest and in danger of attack by predators. The shape of its wings and their pattern of veins make the butterfly look like a dead leaf on a branch. The Indian leaf butterfly also has large spots on its wings, called eyespots. To attacking birds, these look like the eyes of a bigger animal, such as a cat or owl.

## Delicate wings

Like many beetles, the **cockchafer** beetle, or maybug, is an awkward flyer. This is because of its pair of hard wing cases, which it must hold out of the way while it flies. Beetles need these wing cases to protect their thin flying wings when they are crawling on the ground. During flight, cockchafer beetles spread their antennae into a fan. This helps them to sense the direction of the wind, and also to detect the scent of food or a mate.

**Lacewing**
*0.6 in. long*
*Worldwide*

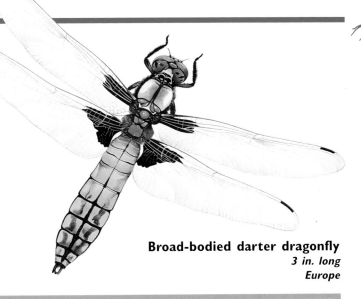

**Broad-bodied darter dragonfly**
*3 in. long*
*Europe*

## Super hearing

**Lacewings** get their name from the network of crisscrossing veins in their delicate wings. They have amazing hearing organs in their wings that allow them to hear the high-pitched squeaks of bats, and so avoid them.

**Passion vine butterfly**
*Wingspan 2.75 in.*
*Central and South America*

## Memorable markings

**Passion vine butterflies** are named for the plants that they eat while they are caterpillars. Harmless to the caterpillars, the passion vine makes the adult butterflies poisonous to other animals. Often, different kinds of passion vine butterflies that live in one area all have very similar patterns and colors. The more alike they look, the safer they are from birds that recall the taste of one of them!

**Bumblebee**
*1 in. long*
*Worldwide*

## Working together

**Bumblebees** live in groups of up to 400 bees, called colonies. A colony begins when the queen bee finds a place such as an old vole's nest, to lay her eggs. The bees that hatch out are the worker bees. It is their job to go out and find food—nectar and pollen.

## Acrobats of the air

**Dragonflies** can fly at great speeds, dart from one direction to another, hover, and even fly backwards. They have enormous eyes that allow them to see in almost any direction. They swoop down on their prey in midair. Dragonflies are usually found around water, where they lay their eggs. The young dragonflies feed on tadpoles, minnows, or small insects. A male dragonfly will often make a stretch of water his own territory.

**Swallowtail**
*Wingspan 4 in.*
*Europe, Asia, North America*

## Slow flyers

**Swallowtail** butterflies have one of the slowest wingbeats of all insects, just five times a second (other insects can reach speeds of hundreds of beats per second). Swallowtail butterfly caterpillars have a very strange disguise when they first hatch. They are black with a white patch in the middle of their bodies, and look very much like bird droppings. When they are older, they are brightly colored, and protect themselves by producing a strong smell.

**Hercules beetle**
**7 in. long**
**South America**

## Amazing insects

I N THE WORLD of insects, there is an incredible range of sizes, shapes, colors, and lifestyles. Pictured on this page are just a few examples of this amazing variety.

The male **hercules beetle** is one of the longest beetles in the world. About half its length is made up of its huge horn which is used to fight other males for mates. Each beetle tries to grab its opponent. Hercules beetles are very strong, and the fight ends when one beetle manages to throw the other onto its back.

The **tsetse fly,** by contrast, is tiny. This illustration of its head *(opposite)* has been magnified many times. The long mouthpart, which has teeth at its tip, is used for piercing the skin of animals and sucking their blood. Tsetse flies may pass on a disease called sleeping sickness to cattle and humans by biting them, too.

**Harlequin longhorn beetle**
**3 in. long**
**South America**

## Puff and hiss

The **hissing cockroach** can measure up to three inches long. Ordinary cockroaches are well-known to many people, and hated because they are pests that live in our houses. However, this cockroach lives in tropical forest on the island of Madagascar. It has a very strange way of protecting itself. When threatened, it fills itself with air to look bigger, and then forces the air out with a loud hissing sound.

**Madagascar hissing cockroach**
**3 in. long**

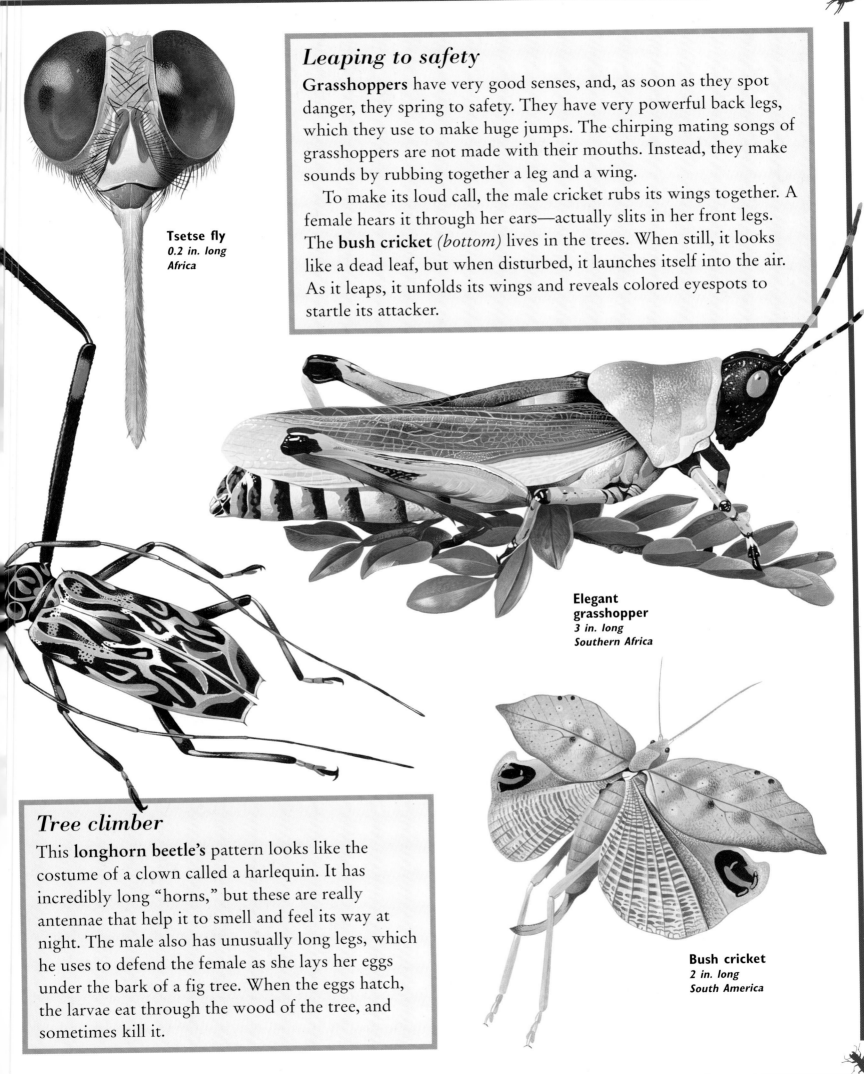

**Tsetse fly**
*0.2 in. long*
*Africa*

## Leaping to safety

**Grasshoppers** have very good senses, and, as soon as they spot danger, they spring to safety. They have very powerful back legs, which they use to make huge jumps. The chirping mating songs of grasshoppers are not made with their mouths. Instead, they make sounds by rubbing together a leg and a wing.

To make its loud call, the male cricket rubs its wings together. A female hears it through her ears—actually slits in her front legs. The **bush cricket** *(bottom)* lives in the trees. When still, it looks like a dead leaf, but when disturbed, it launches itself into the air. As it leaps, it unfolds its wings and reveals colored eyespots to startle its attacker.

**Elegant grasshopper**
*3 in. long*
*Southern Africa*

## Tree climber

This **longhorn beetle's** pattern looks like the costume of a clown called a harlequin. It has incredibly long "horns," but these are really antennae that help it to smell and feel its way at night. The male also has unusually long legs, which he uses to defend the female as she lays her eggs under the bark of a fig tree. When the eggs hatch, the larvae eat through the wood of the tree, and sometimes kill it.

**Bush cricket**
*2 in. long*
*South America*

# Ground bugs mobile

**Millipede**
*1 in. long*
*Temperate worldwide*

**European stag beetle**
*1.6 in. long*

## Leg power

**Millipedes** are well-known for their many pairs of legs—they can have between 40 and 400 of them. These legs are short and strong, enabling millipedes to burrow through soil or vegetation with all their legs moving at once.

## Wrestling match

**Stag beetles** are so called for the huge "horns" of the males. However, these are really massive jaws. They are used when the males fight each other for territory or females. Before the fight, each stands facing the other to see which is the largest. Sometimes, the smaller beetle will decide to give up the challenge. If this does not happen, the beetles lock jaws and wrestle with one another.

**Stick insect**
*3 in. long*
*Worldwide*

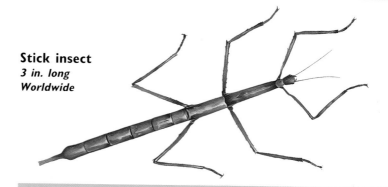

## Swaying twigs

**Stick insects** are experts at the art of camouflage. They sit very still on trees or bushes, and blend in so perfectly you cannot tell them apart from the twigs they are sitting on—a very good defense against predators. They even sway from side to side in a breeze.

**Hawthorn shieldbug**
*0.3–0.5 in. long*
*Temperate Europe and Asia*

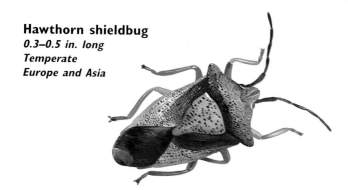

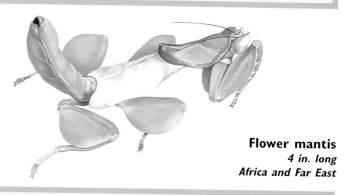

**Flower mantis**
*4 in. long*
*Africa and Far East*

## Good parents

**Shieldbugs** are so called because when their wings are closed, they look like the coat of arms on a shield. They come in all colors and patterns, but, as always, their bright colors tell predators that they are not good to eat. Many types of shieldbug stay with their eggs until hatched, to protect them. If attacked, the shieldbug squirts out a terrible-smelling fluid, sometimes farther than 12 inches. It is no wonder that shieldbugs are often better known as "stinkbugs."

## Deadly flower

The pink, petal-shaped body of the **flower mantis** blends in perfectly with pink orchids. The mantis sits very still among the petals of a flower, and waits for an unsuspecting insect to come by. Sometimes, insects even land on the mantis to try to collect nectar! By the time they discover their mistake, it is too late.

**Dog flea**
*0.1 in. long*
*Worldwide*

**Soldier termite**
*0.3 in. long*
*Tropical and subtropical worldwide*

## Lethal leapers

**Fleas** can survive for months without food, and are fantastic jumpers. They can leap over 100 times their own length (the equivalent of you jumping over the Washington Monument!), and accelerate with more force than a space rocket. Fleas feed on the blood of larger animals like rats or dogs. As they bite, they can pass diseases from sick animals to healthy ones, and even to humans. The most terrible such disease was the plague which killed millions of people in the 14th century.

## Huge jaws

**Termites** live together in vast colonies of thousands. They even have kings and queens, served by armies of workers and soldiers. Soldier termites have the job of protecting the termite colony from invasion. Lining up around the workers, they are ready to snap at any attacker. They have massive heads and huge jaws. Many types of soldier termite have an extra defense against their worst enemies, the ants. They produce a substance that drives the ants away, and can even kill them. However, for all their ferocity, soldier termites are blind, and cannot feed themselves. They must rely on the workers to provide them with food.

**Jumping spider**
*0.1–0.6 in. long*
*Worldwide*

**Ladybug**
*0.3 in. long*
*Temperate worldwide*

## Sharp-eyed hunters

There are thousands of varieties of **jumping spiders**. These tiny spiders do not spin webs, but, as their name suggests, they jump to get from twig to twig, and also to catch their prey. Jumping spiders have a better sense of sight than do any other spiders. Their eight eyes are able to spot movement in any direction around them. They capture their prey by leaping at it with their sharp fangs ready to strike. They often eat moths or flies, but some will attack creatures bigger than themselves, such as the praying mantis.

## The farmer's friend

Everyone knows the **ladybug,** with its red or yellow body and black spots. These bright colors are a warning to any hungry animal that it tastes very bad. If the ladybug senses danger, it reacts by oozing a smelly yellow substance from its leg-joints. This usually drives an attacker away. The ladybug is very useful to gardeners and farmers, because it feeds on tiny pests like aphids that do a lot of damage to crops and plants.

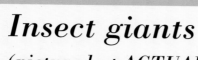

# Insect giants
## (pictured at ACTUAL SIZE)

**Goliath beetle**
*4.5 in. long*
*3.5 oz. in weight*
*Africa*

WHEN WE THINK of insects, we usually imagine the tiny creatures we see every day. However, in some tropical areas of the world, there are insects that grow to spectacular sizes.

The **goliath beetle** is one of the biggest beetles in the world, and can weigh as much as a rat does. In spite of this great weight, it can still fly into the treetops to look for fruit to eat. At night, it crawls under leaves to hide from lizards and other predators.

**Tarantula hawk wasp**
*Wingspan 5 in.*
*Southwest U.S.*

**Giant weta**
*4 in. long*
*New Zealand*

## Fearless

The **tarantula hawk wasp** is the size of a hummingbird. The male wasp is harmless, but the female is a deadly hunter of tarantula spiders. As the spider rears up to strike at her, she stings it. Then she drags the spider into a hole, where she lays an egg on it.

The **giant weta,** from an island off New Zealand, is a cricketlike insect. However, it is about four times the size of an ordinary cricket. If threatened, it kicks out with its long, spiny back legs. This huge creature is a protected species.

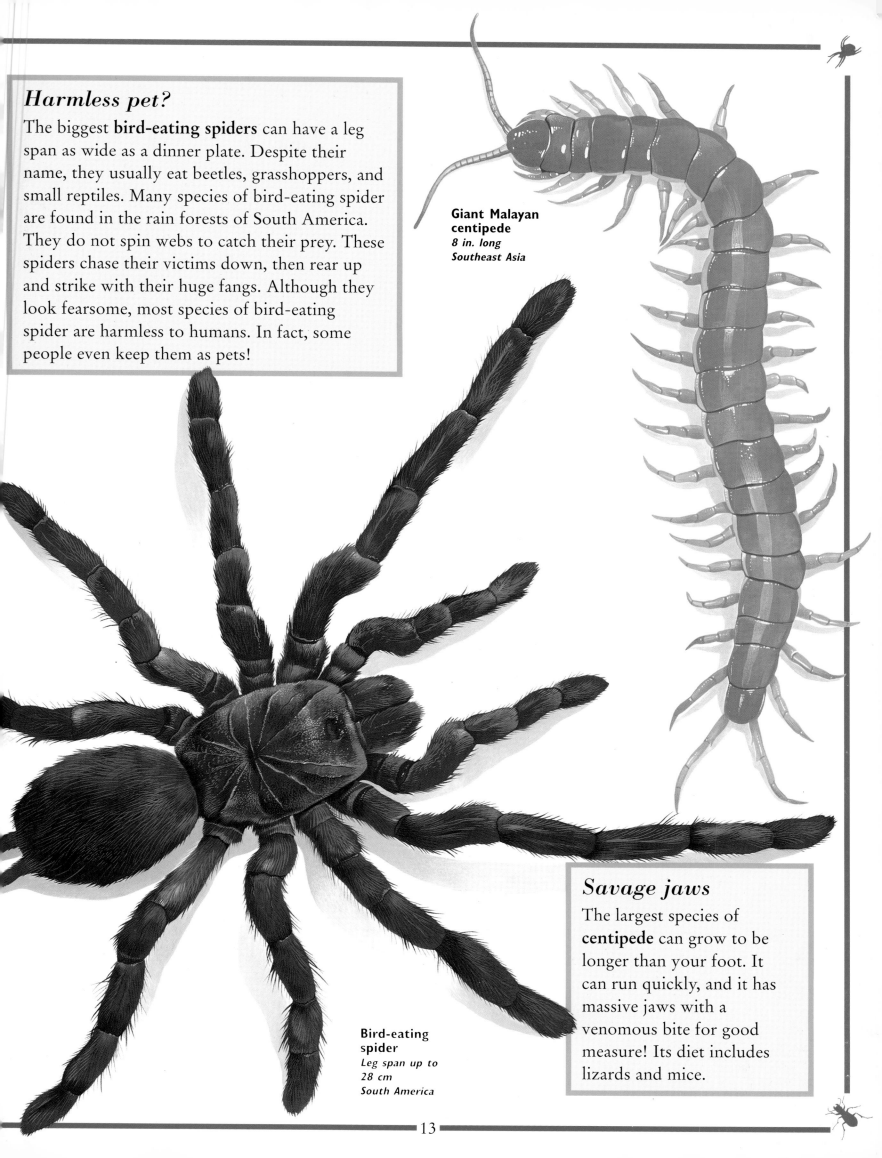

## Harmless pet?

The biggest **bird-eating spiders** can have a leg span as wide as a dinner plate. Despite their name, they usually eat beetles, grasshoppers, and small reptiles. Many species of bird-eating spider are found in the rain forests of South America. They do not spin webs to catch their prey. These spiders chase their victims down, then rear up and strike with their huge fangs. Although they look fearsome, most species of bird-eating spider are harmless to humans. In fact, some people even keep them as pets!

**Giant Malayan
centipede**
*8 in. long
Southeast Asia*

**Bird-eating
spider**
*Leg span up to
28 cm
South America*

## Savage jaws

The largest species of **centipede** can grow to be longer than your foot. It can run quickly, and it has massive jaws with a venomous bite for good measure! Its diet includes lizards and mice.

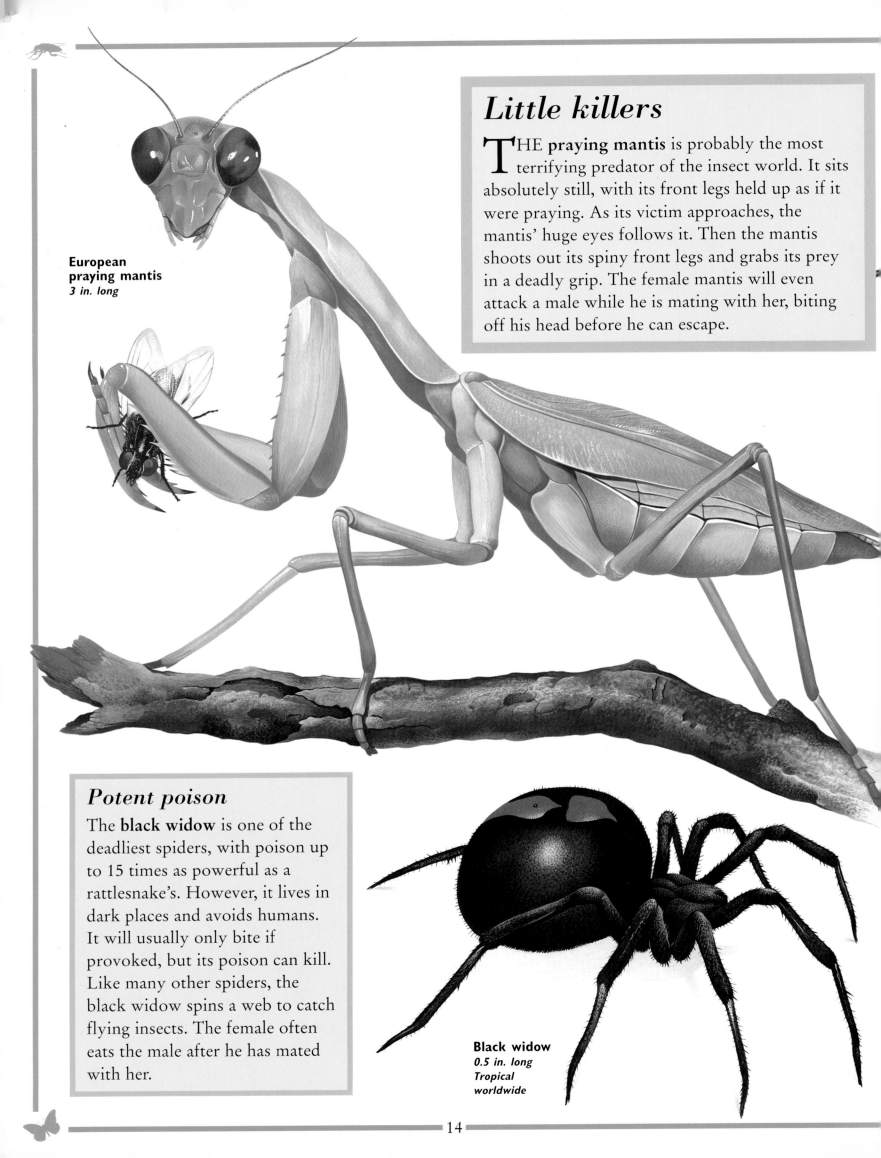

**European praying mantis**
*3 in. long*

## Little killers

THE **praying mantis** is probably the most terrifying predator of the insect world. It sits absolutely still, with its front legs held up as if it were praying. As its victim approaches, the mantis' huge eyes follows it. Then the mantis shoots out its spiny front legs and grabs its prey in a deadly grip. The female mantis will even attack a male while he is mating with her, biting off his head before he can escape.

## Potent poison

The **black widow** is one of the deadliest spiders, with poison up to 15 times as powerful as a rattlesnake's. However, it lives in dark places and avoids humans. It will usually only bite if provoked, but its poison can kill. Like many other spiders, the black widow spins a web to catch flying insects. The female often eats the male after he has mated with her.

**Black widow**
*0.5 in. long*
*Tropical worldwide*

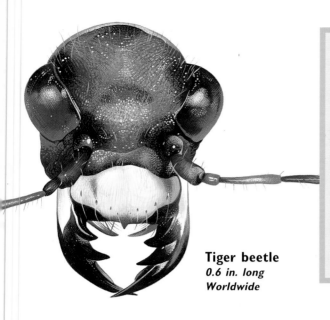

**Tiger beetle**
*0.6 in. long*
*Worldwide*

## Advancing army

**Army ants** march steadily through the rain forest undergrowth killing anything in their path. There can be hundreds of thousands of ants in one colony, and they form a pack up to 30 feet wide. In some villages, people flee their homes while the ants pass through.

**Army ant**
*0.1 in. long*
*Central and*
*South America*

## No escape

The **tiger beetle** is a fierce predator—both as an adult and a larva. The tiger beetle larva hides at the top of its burrow, and grabs any passing insect in its jaws. The adult beetle chases and catches its prey out in the open. This greatly magnified illustration of the beetle's head *(above)* shows its powerful jaws. It is one of the fastest insects on the ground: A tiger beetle the same size as a cheetah could easily beat it in a race.

The **great diving beetle** is just as good at swimming as at flying. It lives in ponds and streams, and can even breathe underwater. The beetle grabs its prey with its front legs, then eats it. Even small fish cannot escape its clutches.

**European hornet**
*0.75-1.5 in. long*
*Europe and Asia*

**Great diving beetle**
*2.6 in. long*
*Worldwide*

## Bad temper

The **hornet's** yellow and black colors are well-known and avoided by both other animals and people. A number of insects even try to look like it to avoid being eaten. Hornets sting when their nest is attacked or threatened. The sting is painful for humans, but deadly to smaller insects.

# Index

The Big Book of Mobiles: Bugs
Published by Time-Life Books

Time-Life Books is a division of
TIME LIFE INCORPORATED

Time-Life Custom Publishing
*Vice President and Publisher:* Terry Newell
*Project Manager:* Christopher M. Register
*Director of New Product Development:* Regina Hall
*Director of Sales:* Neil Levin
*Managing Editor:* Donia Ann Steele

Books produced by Time-Life Custom Publishing are available at special
bulk discount for promotional and premium use. Custom adaptations can
also be created to meet your specific marketing goals.

1-800-323-5255

Created and produced by Orpheus Books Ltd

*Text:* Claire Aston
*Illustrator:* David Wright *(Kathy Jakeman Illustration)*
*Consultants:* Dr Christopher O' Toole, Hope
  Entomological Collections of the University Museum,
  Oxford, England
  Carol Sheppard, Department of Entomology, Washington
  State University
*Editorial and design:* Nicholas Harris
*Production:* Joanna Turner

© Orpheus Books Ltd 1997

ISBN 0-7835-4886-9

Printed and bound in Singapore